What is a Forest?

Monica Hughes

Sch

www.raintreepublishers.co.uk
Visit our website to find out more information about **Raintree** books.

To order:
☎ Phone 44 (0) 1865 888112
📄 Send a fax to 44 (0) 1865 314091
💻 Visit the Raintree Bookshop at **www.raintreepublishers.co.uk** to browse our catalogue and order online.

First published in Great Britain by Raintree, Halley Court, Jordan Hill, Oxford OX2 8EJ, part of Harcourt Education.
Raintree is a registered trademark of Harcourt Education Ltd.

Editorial: Catherine Clarke and Sarah Chappelow
Design: Michelle Lisseter
Picture Research: Maria Joannou, Erica Newbery and Kay Altwegg
Production: Amanda Meaden

Originated by Dot Gradations Ltd
Printed and bound in China by South China Printing Company

ISBN 1 844 43645 4 (hardback)
09 08 07 06 05
10 9 8 7 6 5 4 3 2 1

ISBN 1 844 43651 9 (paperback)
10 09 08 07 06
10 9 8 7 6 5 4 3 2 1

British Library Cataloguing in Publication Data
Hughes, Monica
What is a Forest?. – (The World Around Us)
577.3
A full catalogue record for this book is available from the British Library.

Acknowledgements
The publishers would like to thank the following for permission to reproduce photographs: Alamy p. 21; Corbis pp. 5 (Paul A. Souders), 7, 11, 12 (Layne Kennedy), 13 (Mary Ann McDonald), 15 (Chinch Gryniewicz/Ecoscene), 16 (Layne Kennedy) 23f; Digital Vision pp. 17, 22, 23d; Getty Images pp. 4, (Photodisc), 10 (Photodisc), 22 (Photodisc), 22 (Digital Vision) 23e (Photodisc); Harcourt Education Ltd (Corbis) pp. 8, 14, 22, 23b; NHPA pp. 6 (Guy Edwardes), 18, 19 (Simon Booth) 23c (Simon Booth), 22; Photodisc pp. 9, 20, 23a.

Cover photograph reproduced with permission of Harcourt Education Ltd (Corbis).

Every effort has been made to contact copyright holders of any material reproduced in this book. Any omissions will be rectified in subsequent printings if notice is given to the publishers.

The paper used to print this book comes from sustainable resources.

Contents

Some words are shown in bold, **like this.**
You can find them in the glossary on page 23.

Have you seen a forest?

A forest is a place where there are lots of trees.

There are forests all over the world.

Forests are not all the same.

Some are in cold places and some are in hot places.

What is a forest like in spring?

In **temperate** places spring is when everything starts to grow.

Trees grow new leaves and bluebells might cover the ground.

As warmer weather comes, the trees are covered with leaves.

Some forests have trees covered in leaves all year round.

What is a forest like in autumn?

In a **deciduous** forest the trees change in autumn.

The leaves turn red, orange, and yellow and fall from the trees.

In a **coniferous** forest the trees are evergreen.

The trees never lose their leaves, and stay green even in winter.

What does a forest feel like?

In a **temperate** forest it feels cool under the trees.

The trees give shade and the ground can feel damp.

In a **tropical** forest it feels hot and sticky, even in the shade.

After rain, the leaves drip with water.

What does a forest sound like?

Autumn leaves can make a rustling sound.

The leaves crunch and crackle when they are walked on.

Different birds can be heard singing in the trees.

It may even be possible to hear the tap, tapping of a woodpecker.

How big is a forest?

The trees in some forests can be much taller than a house.

Young trees and other plants can be very small.

Some forests are so big it would take days to walk through them.

The forest spreads as new trees grow.

What animals live in forests?

Different animals live in different types of forest.

Deer live in **temperate** forests. So do foxes, badgers, and rabbits.

Trees in **tropical** forests are home to monkeys, **orang-utans**, and lots of birds.

Tigers also live in some forests.

What else lives in a forest?

The forest floor is home to tiny creatures such as ants and spiders.

Creatures like woodlice feed on tree trunks or rotten plants.

Flowers and climbing plants live in forests.

Fungi such as toadstools feed on rotting trees.

How do people use forests?

Trees can be cut down to make furniture or paper.

Some forests are grown especially for their wood.

Many people enjoy visiting forests
to see trees, plants, or animals.

Forests are also enjoyed by walkers
and mountain bikers.

Quiz

Which of these animals live in a forest?

Glossary

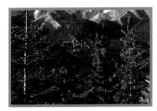

coniferous
having trees with needle-like leaves and cones. Coniferous trees do not lose their leaves in autumn.

deciduous
having trees that shed their leaves in autumn

fungi
living thing that is like a plant, without leaves, flowers, or roots. Mushrooms and toadstools are fungi.

orang-utan
large ape with long red hair and long arms. Orang-utans live in trees.

temperate
neither very hot or very cold

tropical
always very hot and rainy

Index

Answer to quiz on page 22

Woodlice, orang-utans, and deer all live in forests.